Sol Luna Flor

Poems of Life's Seasons and Rotations

V.M. Fresquez

India | USA | UK

Dedication

Dedicated to love, nature, and the love of nature.
May they never part.

Preface

This collection of poems is a handful of many. I have scribbled down poetic inspirations most of my life. I would always say, "someday I am going to put a book together!" That time has come. Sometimes, it's about timing and opportunities, or maybe a blood moon. In any case, the door opened, and I walked through. My dream is that this book is just the beginning. This one is my first bloom of spring. These poems are simple feelings and experiences I have encountered with nature, love, and life.

It's hard to narrow down what you'll share and to know what it will stir. I hope that this collection will speak directly to your heart in a way that evokes nostalgia, longing, and sweet reverie. Poems come to me when I find myself in awe, and I manage to capture the moment in words. It would be nice if I could photograph a feeling, a smell, or maybe a visceral memory. Words are my camera in these cases, poetry my stories, my songs.

Acknowledgements

To my precious partner and biggest supporter, Natalie. Thank you for believing in me and my visions, for listening to all my dreams, and for reminding me that I am enough. You always find ways to lift me up and encourage me to be true to myself. Listening to my Sagittarius ramblings, can be no easy feat for a focused Capricorn, but your love and dedication makes space for it all. Thank you! I love you always.

Not to be forgotten, our third beating heart. The love of our lives, little Winnie. The most strong-spirited little dog there ever was. She completes us and I am obsessed.

Sol Luna Flor.

I'm here to love you
Know your dreams
Note your fears
Make your life grand and full
To keep you calm and smiling
My calling is clear
Through storms and rainbows
I'll be here
Always at your side
To be sure you bask in golden light

Sol Luna Flor.

You're a rose
Grow your thorns
Soft gentle beauty
Sacred, protected
Bloom in your power
Stand tall and strong
Toothed leaves
Razor thin
Warm in the sun
Fiery in the rain
Ablaze with love
Quiet joy
Prideful refrain
Surely alluring
Softly independent

Sol Luna Flor.

Meteor out of heaven
A cast line
Fishing for angels
Bound to earth
Crashing into me
Knocked to my knees
I've fallen, I'm hooked
Lured by dazzling eyes
Surprised by the flash
Of your blinding smile
Our hearts connected tightly
Fused into many colors dancing
Sizzling stars and moons
Igniting the night
Any time before you is gone
A pink cloud floating away
Cotton candy I once ate
Something I vaguely remember fondly
Now is everything
And you are all of it

Sol Luna Flor.

Have I ever mentioned how much I love you?
I can spend hours doing nothing
Just so you can sleep
So I can smell your sweet little scent
So our hearts can beat together
Our souls reminisce
The warmth we share
Intertwining our dreams
You were heaven sent
I am your guardian
You are my pet

Sol Luna Flor.

Somehow you knew
And welcomed me in
An offering of comfort
Maybe I needed it
Or you did
Or both
Strange moment
Tender surprise
I don't understand
But I'll just let it go by
Love is that way
Reaching without consent
No explanation for why
Head on your chest
A soft letting go
Of what I don't know

Sol Luna Flor.

You loved me so much
Broke me right open
Cracks in my armor shattered
My deepest secrets found
The light inside pouring out
I was a stump
Leveled to the ground
You sang to me
Held me
Believed in my revival
You made me want to win
To live up to your faith
I wanted you to glow
Like you did when I smiled at you
I felt your heart rescuing me
I held on tight
So did you
Together we survived

Sol Luna Flor.

Beneath rays of a golden sun
The heart of a turquoise sky
Tucked away between grasslands and mountains
Mesas and desert
There is a land of enchantment
At one with spirits and stars
Attuned to the four winds
Spring through winter
From birth to goodbye
A circle of love and life going round
No beginning, no end
Eternally weaving the story of life
The dream of existence
New Mexico

Sol Luna Flor.

Running away with the wind
Flowers in my hair
Hovering above the ground
Catching air
Drunken crazy fool!
Entrapped by wild bouquets
Wafting, wrapping, whirling around me
I go faster
Into my future
On the wings of my present
Behind me a dream come true

Sol Luna Flor.

And so it unfolds
Your future glaring in the sun
Alive, active, churning
Invisible steps appear
One by one
Before you in a sea of eternity
A bridge to the path of the rest of your life
Bravely you answer the call
Stepping forward
Going strongly into the dense fog
Unsure, unknowing
Scared but trusting

Sol Luna Flor.

Mullein
Regal and tall between the pine
Evergreen
Yarrow swaying softly
Ever so slight
Aspen quaking in the sun
Waving farewell as we pass by
Mountain tops pressed against the sky
Clouds pushing against sharp peaks
Eagles soar
Magpies fly

Sol Luna Flor.

Sea spray across my lips
Mist freckling my face
Orange crush summer
Sun-kissed L.A. day
Pelicans dipping and diving
Seagulls soaring with waves
Roaring swells
Puffy rolls
Hurling towards me
Hello's from far and deep
I'm home and it tastes sweet

Sol Luna Flor.

I love you both
No comparison
One bare and smooth
Dotted by creosote bush
Bougainvillea bright as starfish in the sun
The other rugged and rough
Whispering meadows sway
Endless starry skies billowing
With each of you I am whole

Sol Luna Flor.

She would always say
"Love you bunches and bunches mi hita"
I could never forget her warm hugs or
Twinkling lite-brite eyes
Her spirit was big and strong
She was petite and mighty
A butterfly, a lady bug
A wonderful woman
She saved me so many times
Forgave me for being young and silly
She could not have loved me better
And I will love and miss her
Forever more
My grandma

Sol Luna Flor.

Quick little rainstorm
Over my heart
Cloudy sky
Lighting strikes
A flood of tears
Hailing hard against my cheeks
Flubbering lips
Thundering sheets of pain
Crackle down my spine
Memories whipping at my eyes
I remember your face
Your smile
Your vibe
The sun returns
I grow another leaf
Another petal
Another flower
I bloom

Sol Luna Flor.

Oh rain
Absorb my tears
Whisk them away
Clear the pain
I cannot take
Wash me clean
Refresh my faith
Make me new again
So my heart can chance another stake

Sol Luna Flor.

Forever smiling
Forever crying
Tears of a clown
Soft places inside
Slowly expiring
One last whisper
A final breath
Weeping willow
Bleeding heart
Butterfly in my chest
Nose to hyacinth
Awaken my senses!
Without love
I'm not my best
Weakening pulse quicken!
We've work to do
Dances to dance
Jokes to tell
The show must go on my friend

Sol Luna Flor.

Blue Jay in the tree
Ducks in the creek
Squirrel shoring up her nest
Fish racing down stream
Cottonwood buds scattered
Mixed with blankets of leaves
I'm just me
A Violet perched quietly
On a boulder
Feeling lucky to have a seat
At the table of her majesty
Our Mother
Earth

Sol Luna Flor.

Because I know you
I know a giraffe
Long, soft neck
Bambi brown spots

Because I know you
I know a rabbit
Big, round eyes
Soft, slender ears

Because I know you
I know a cat
Cuddles against my legs
Stretching across my body

I see you in all of them
Wild and free
Strong and resilient
Docile when they want to be
The way it is between you and me

Sol Luna Flor.

We dream of flowers
They dream of us
A bond of trust
Family knowledge
That can't be lost

Sol Luna Flor.

In the trastero, a comal
To make tortillas for dinner
Caldito and pepinos
Red chile and beans
Maybe calabacitas and corn
Familia gathers for meals
Together we cook, we eat, we clean
Estropajos for wiping tables
Toallitas for hands
The hielera ready for leftovers
Manana otra vez
My youth colored in Spanglish
Chicano pride
American dreams
Spanish roots
Mestiza flor
El sol my guide
La Luna my soul
Always calling me home

Sol Luna Flor.

Many hours a day
I drift
Far away fantasies
Streaming through sunbeams
Aimlessly
Happy wanderer
Swept away

www.ingramcontent.com/pod-product-compliance
Lightning Source LLC
LaVergne TN
LVHW050504210726
843509LV00015BA/2997